discover countries

Discover India

Tim Atkinson

PowerKiDS press.

New York

Published in 2012 by The Rosen Publishing Group Inc.
29 East 21st Street, New York, NY 10010

Editor: Paul Manning
Designer: Paul Manning
Consultants: Rob Bowden, Sanjay Patel

Library of Congress Cataloging-in-Publication Data

Atkinson, Tim.
Discover India / by Tim Atkinson. — 1st ed.
    p. cm. — (Discover countries)
Includes index.
ISBN 978-1-4488-5268-0 (library binding)
1. India—Juvenile literature. I. Title.
DS407.A785 2012
954—dc22

                         2010046124

Photographs:
Cover l, Shutterstock/Vishal Shah; cover r, 26, Shutterstock/Jarno Gonzalez Zarraonandia;
1, Shutterstock/Vishal Shah; 3t, Shutterstock/Wong Yu Liang; 3m, Shutterstock/Oksana Perkins; 3b, Shutterstock/Arteki; 4,
map) Stefan Chabluk; 5, Shutterstock/Arteki; 6, Corbis/Hans Georg Roth; 7, Corbis/Jon Hicks; 8, Corbis/Caroline Penn; 9,
Corbis/E.P.A.; 10, Corbis/Frèdèric Soltan; 11, Shutterstock/Vishal Shah; 12, Shutterstock/Zeber; 13, Shutterstock/Tian Zhan;
14, Shutterstock/Ricardo Miguel; 15, Corbis/Bob Krist; 16, Corbis/Pallava Bagla; 17, Corbis/Marco Cristofori; 18, Corbis/Amit
Bhargava; 19, Corbis/Desmond Boylan; 20, Corbis/Ed Kashi; 21t, Shutterstock/Blueee; 21b, Shutterstock/Paul Prescott;
22, Corbis/Wolfgang Langenstrassen; 23b, Shutterstock/Paul Prescott; 24, Wikimedia/Picasa; 25, Shutterstock/Paul Prescott;
27, Corbis/Amit Dave; 28, Shutterstock/Tan Kian Khoon; 29a, Shutterstock/Mikhail Nekrasov; 29b, Corbis/Robert Wallis.

All data in this book was researched in 2009 and has been collected from the latest sources available at that time.

Manufactured in China
CPSIA Compliance Information: Batch # WAS1102PK: For Further Information contact Rosen Publishing, New York, New York at 1-800-237-9932

Contents

Discovering India

India is the seventh-largest country in the world by area and has the world's second-largest population after China. Over the last ten years, India's economy has boomed and its cities have grown rapidly—but because of its huge population, many Indian people still live in poverty.

An Ancient Civilization

India is one of the world's oldest civilizations. In the Indus Valley region of northwest India, people lived in towns and cities as long ago as 2600 BCE.

During the eighth century CE, raiders from Arab countries began to occupy parts of India, and from 1526, Mughal emperors from central Asia ruled much of the country. From the seventeenth century onward, India's natural riches attracted European traders. By the mid-eighteenth century, Great Britain's East India Company controlled the region, and in 1858, India became part of the British Empire.

India Statistics

Area: 2 million sq. miles (3.3 million sq. km)

Capital city: New Delhi

Government type: Federal Republic

Bordering countries: Bangladesh, Bhutan, Burma, China, Nepal, Pakistan

Currency: Indian rupee

Languages: Hindi 41%, Bengali 8.1%, Telugu 7.2%, Marathi 7%, Tamil 5.9%, Urdu 5%, Gujarati 4.5%, Kannada 3.7%, Malayalam 3.2%, Oriya 3.2%, Punjabi 2.8%, Assamese 1.3%, Maithili 1.2%, other 5.9%

India and Pakistan

After a long campaign of civil disobedience led by Mahatma Gandhi (1869–1948), India broke free from Britain in 1947 to become an independent nation. At the same time, Muslim areas were divided to form the smaller states of East and West Pakistan. In 1971, East Pakistan split from West Pakistan to form the separate nation of Bangladesh.

Modern India

India's national government is based in the capital, New Delhi. The country is governed by the prime minister and cabinet, with an elected president acting as head of state. Following elections in 2009, the Congress Party, under its leader Dr. Manmohan Singh, was returned to power with an increased majority.

A Dynamic Economy

With its skilled workforce and low labor costs, India has one of the fastest-growing economies in the world. Though the country's population remains largely rural, India has three of the most populous cities in the world—Mumbai, Kolkata, and Delhi. Three other Indian cities, Bangalore, Chennai, and Hyderabad, are among the world's fastest-growing high-technology centers. Most of the world's major information technology and software companies now have offices in India.

▼ Known as the Lotus Temple because of its flowerlike shape, the Baha'i Temple in Delhi is one of the most visited places of worship in India.

Landscape and Climate

The Indian subcontinent was formed millions of years ago by the shifting and colliding of the vast plates of rock that form the Earth's crust. To the south, India forms a triangular peninsula jutting into the Indian Ocean. To the north, it is bordered by the world's highest mountain range, the Himalayas.

A Varied Landscape

India's landscape includes mountains, deserts, river plains, and hilly, tropical forests. In the Himalayas, the same forces that shaped the mountains millions of years ago still cause earthquakes and landslides. In 2000, an earth tremor in Gujarat state claimed the lives of more than 20,000 people and left more than 500,000 homeless.

▼ In the Himalayas the temperature changes rapidly. Sudden monsoons, floods, high winds, and snowstorms make this one of the harshest environments on Earth.

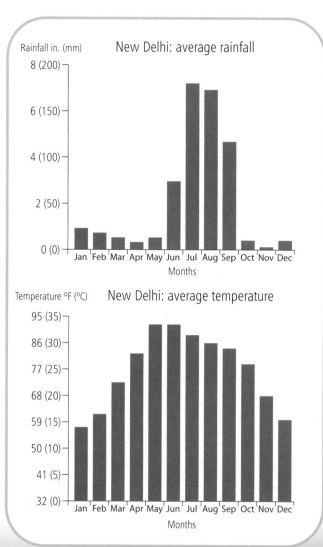

New Delhi: average rainfall

Rainfall in. (mm)

New Delhi: average temperature

Temperature °F (°C)

The fertile North Indian Plain is dominated by the Ganges River, which rises in the Himalayas and flows eastward into the Bay of Bengal.

India's southern peninsula is mostly mountainous. On the western side, the Western Ghats rise steeply from the coastal plain. Heavy rains fall on the Deccan Plateau, feeding major rivers such as the Krishna, Godavari, and Kaveri, which flow out through the Eastern Ghats and into the Bay of Bengal.

A Monsoon Climate

In India, temperatures vary from region to region. In Lucknow in Uttar Pradesh, summer temperatures can hit 118°F (48°C), while winter in Kashmir in northwestern India can be as cold as –49 °F (–45 °C).

India's climate is dominated by strong winds called monsoons that change direction with the season.

India's winters are mostly hot and dry. The monsoon winds blow from the northeast and carry little moisture. The temperature is high because the Himalayas form a barrier that prevents cold air from passing onto the subcontinent.

Monsoon Rains

In summer, the winds come from the southwest, picking up water from the Indian Ocean. These winds bring heavy rains from May to October, providing 80 percent of India's annual rainfall.

The monsoon rains are vital to India, because the water fills the rivers that are used for drinking water, for watering crops, and for generating electricity. Without the rain, rivers would run dry and crops would fail.

⬓ The Ganges River drains a 390,000-sq. mile (1,000,000-sq. km) basin stretching from Haridwar in the west to Bangladesh. Nearly 400 million Indians depend on the Ganges to irrigate their crops.

Facts at a Glance

Land area: 1.8 million sq. miles (2.9 million sq. km)

Water area: 121,391 sq. miles (314,400 sq. km)

Highest point: Kanchenjunga, 28,209 ft. (8,598 m)

Lowest point: Indian Ocean, 0 ft. (0 m)

Longest river: Ganges, 1,560 miles (2,510 km)

Coastline: 4,350 miles (7,000 km)

DID YOU KNOW?

Cherrapunji in northeast India is one of the wettest places on earth. Its annual rainfall is 35.4 ft. (10,798 mm). In 1861, it had its wettest monsoon ever, recording 75 ft. (22,625 mm) of rain.

Population and Health

In 2001, India's population became the second in the world after China to exceed one billion. If its present birth rate of 1.65 percent continues, by 2050, India is expected to overtake China to become the most populous country in the world.

A Mixed Population

At different times in its history, people from different parts of the world including Arabs, Turks, Mongols, and Afghans have settled in India and intermarried. Because of this, India's population is more ethnically mixed than almost any other nation in the world. Every state contains countless different minority groups, each with their own culture, language, and identity.

The Hindu Caste System

Hindu people belong to groups known as castes. In a traditional caste system, people must stay in the position and role into which they are born and not marry outside their community.

In the past, members of the lowest castes were shunned by the rest of society. Today caste barriers are slowly disappearing and people called *dalits,* who belong to the lowest castes, receive special help from the government.

⬥ Indian women learn how to maintain their village water pump. Access to clean water is a major health issue in India. Many people die of diseases caused by dirty water and lack of basic sanitation.

Facts at a Glance

Total population: 1.2 billion

Life expectancy at birth: 70 years

Children dying before the age of five: 7.4%

Ethnic composition: Indo-Aryan 72%, Dravidian 25%, Mongoloid and other 3%

A Healthier India?

Since 1945, life expectancy in India has risen by more than 25 years. New hospitals and vaccination programs are helping to stamp out diseases that once claimed the lives of millions.

But as health and living standards improve and people in India live longer, the pressures of overpopulation become even greater. Each year India's population grows by an estimated 17 million people. This puts a huge strain on India's health and welfare system. The UN estimates that 2.1 million Indian children below the age of five die every year, mostly from preventable illnesses such as diarrhea, typhoid, malaria, measles, and pneumonia.

▼ Indian mothers wait for their babies to be innoculated with vaccines supplied by the children's aid organization UNICEF.

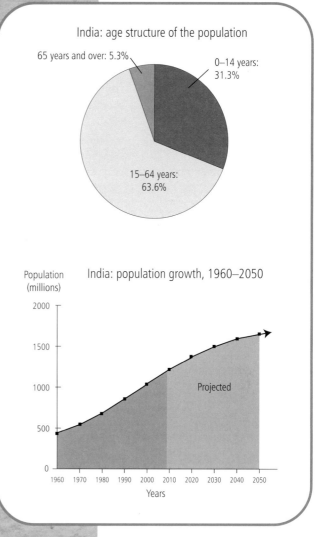

India: age structure of the population

65 years and over: 5.3%

0–14 years: 31.3%

15–64 years: 63.6%

India: population growth, 1960–2050

Population (millions)

Projected

Years

DID YOU KNOW?
Indian medicine dates back to the first millennium BCE. Many of its methods, such as the use of herbs and massage, are now practiced by "alternative therapists" in the West.

Settlements and Living

Apart from remote parts of the Himalayas, almost every corner of India is inhabited. Three-quarters of the population live in rural areas and half survive by growing their own crops. In the cities, the population is growing fast, and 40 Indian cities now have a population of more than a million.

India's Growing Cities

Most of India's towns and cities are in the more prosperous northwest, west, and south of the country.

Mumbai is India's largest city with a population of 19 million. Since the 1970s, Mumbai has experienced a building boom and is one of the world's fastest-growing cities. New Delhi, India's capital, is the next largest city, with a population of 16 million. Kolkata, the former capital, has a population of 14.8 million.

Facts at a Glance

Urban population: 28.7% (325.6 million)

Rural population: 71.3% (808.8 million)

Population of largest city: 19 million (Mumbai)

▼ A luxury development of high-rise apartment buildings at Powai in northern Mumbai.

Urban Sprawl

In many of India's cities, rapid population growth, combined with people moving to urban areas in search of work, has created huge problems. In Mumbai the wealthy live in luxury modern apartments, but poor people cannot afford even a modest home.

More than one and a half million people in New Delhi live in *bastis* (shanty towns) on the outskirts of the city. In Mumbai and even n new cities like Chandigarh, there are many homeless people, and large numbers live on the streets, without access to food, clean water, and basic shelter.

India population: rural/urban split, 1960–2050

Population in urban area (%)

Projected

Years

Rural Areas

In rural India, life depends on water and soil to grow crops. In Kerala in southwest India, where water is plentiful and soils are fertile, there are 2,000 persons to each square mile (800 per square kilometer)— nearly three times as many as in other parts of the country. The rich soils of the Ganges plain are intensively cultivated and support some of the highest-density populations in the world.

DID YOU KNOW?
The Banjari are a group of people similar to European gypsies who have no permanent home. They roam all over central India, earning a living from construction work and working on farms.

Village Life

In Indian villages, water is usually supplied from a well, which is often away from the houses to reduce the risk of waterborne diseases. Houses are built of brick or mud, often with a thatched or tiled roof. In areas prone to flooding, houses sometimes stand on piles above the ground.

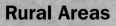
Traditional houses in a village in rural India.

Family Life

In many parts of India, family life has hardly changed for centuries. In rural areas, people live mostly in extended families, with grandparents, parents, and children sharing the same house. In the cities, nuclear families are becoming more common, but even when families live apart, ties between family members are strong.

Family Roles

In a typical Indian household, money, property, and food are all shared. Family members share the same house and often run small businesses together in the family home.

Family roles are strictly laid down. The oldest male acts as head of the family. Wives are expected to obey their husbands. In some communities, women are not allowed to remarry after their husbands die, even if they are widowed at a young age.

▶ In India, every child is seen as a blessing on the household. Sons are especially valued since they will continue the family line and provide for their parents in their old age.

Traditionally, men go out to work to support the family, and women take care of the household chores, but in cities, more and more women are taking jobs. Among wealthier families, women who have jobs often employ domestic workers to do household tasks.

Getting Married

Because of India's caste system, marriage partners in rural India nearly always come from the same village or community. Most marriages are arranged by the family of the bride and groom. Sometimes the family will consult a professional matchmaker to find a suitable partner.

⚫ At a Hindu wedding ceremony, the bride (second from the left) prepares to meet her husband for the first time.

Traditionally, when a Hindu girl gets married, her father is expected to make a gift called a dowry to the groom's family. For a poor family, this is often a lot of money to find. Many Indians feel that this practice is out of date and puts an unfair burden on families.

Children and Seniors

Because family units are often large, there are usually plenty of people to help with the care of young children. Grandparents and unmarried women relatives may all take part in raising children in return for living in the family home. Older relatives are highly respected, and are taken care of by other family members.

Facts at a Glance

Average children per childbearing woman:
2.7 children

Average household size:
5.3 people

Religion and Beliefs

Religion has been part of India's culture for thousands of years. Three of the world's great religions—Buddhism, Sikhism, and Hinduism—originated in India, and many religions that developed in other countries are widely practiced by Indian people.

A Secular State

When India became independent in 1947, the country became a secular state and all religions were given equal status in law. This was an important step to protect religious minorities. Although there are still tensions between Hindus and Muslims, religious tolerance is an important principle in India.

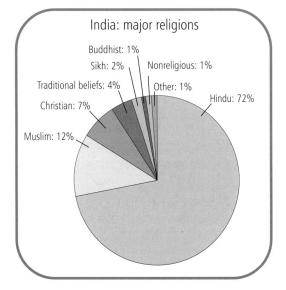

India: major religions

Buddhist: 1%
Sikh: 2%
Nonreligious: 1%
Traditional beliefs: 4%
Other: 1%
Christian: 7%
Hindu: 72%
Muslim: 12%

▶ The Ganges is a holy river to Hindus and bathing in its waters is believed to wash away sins.

India's Many Faiths

Over 80 percent of people in India are Hindus, but India's 120-million-strong Muslim population is one of the largest in the world. The country has large numbers of Christians, Buddhists, and Sikhs, as well as followers of an ancient religion known as Jainism. India is one of the few countries where the Persian religion of Zoroastrianism is still followed.

Sacred Cows

Hinduism is the oldest of India's religions, dating back to 1500 BCE. Hindus respect all forms of life, and the cow is considered a holy animal. In Indian towns and villages, it is not uncommon to see a cow wandering the streets, decked with flowers and free to roam wherever it likes.

The Ganges River—Ganga Maia or "Mother Ganges"—is also sacred to Hindus, and its source high in the Himalayas is a place of pilgrimage. Every year thousands of Hindus gather at Varanasi, on the banks of the Ganges, to visit shrines and ritually cleanse themselves in the river.

Hindu Festivals

Religious festivals are an important part of Indian life. Most take place between October and March. Diwali, also known as the "festival of lights," marks the start of the Hindu New Year and is celebrated by lighting lamps and exchanging gifts. Holi marks the beginning of spring, when Indians traditionally celebrate by throwing colored water and powder at each other, commemorating the pranks played by the young god Krishna.

DID YOU KNOW? The Hindu temple at Deshnoke in Rajasthan is dedicated to rats, which are believed to represent the souls of ancestors. Temple devotees protect them and even share their meals with them.

⬤ A young girl sells candles and gifts for the Hindu festival of Diwali.

Education and Learning

Over the past 60 years, access to education in India has risen and free education is now available for all children between the ages of six and 14. However, school attendance is not compulsory. About 10 percent of Indian children do not go to school at all, and many of those who do attend school leave before the age of 11.

School Attendance

In India, elementary schools cater for children of six to 11, and secondary schools for students ages 14 to 17. Higher education includes technical schools, colleges, and universities. Hindi and English are the main languages of instruction, but local languages are also spoken.

Facts at a Glance

Children in elementary school: Male 90%, Female 87%

Children in secondary school: Male (not available) Female 43%

Literacy rate (over 15 years): 61%

▼ Children at a primary school in India's Tamil Nadu region. In India, class sizes range from 40 to 60 pupils per teacher.

The Gender Gap

Most Indian children enroll in elementary school, but not all attend regularly. In rural areas, some children find it hard to get to school because of lack of transportation. Many girls miss going to school because their parents do not believe that daughters need to be as well educated as sons, or because they are needed to care for siblings.

After elementary school, the gap between boys and girls becomes even wider. In 2006, roughly 10 percent fewer girls than boys attended secondary school. Currently, only 39 percent of Indian women go on to higher education.

Promoting Women's Education

Until recently, Indian parents had to pay to send their children to secondary school. However, to encourage more girls to stay at school, the Indian government has introduced free education for girls over the age of 14.

State governments are also employing more female teachers, providing free books and uniforms and updating school textbooks to provide girls with more positive role models.

Higher Education

India's higher education system is the third largest in the world after China and the United States, with 235 universities and 16,000 colleges. Most students pay tuition fees, but some universities offer free places to women students.

Around 4,000 students a year enroll at India's Institutes of Technology (IITs), which are among the top training grounds for scientists and engineers in Asia. Many IIT graduates go on to find well-paid work in other countries. An estimated 30,000 are employed in the software industry in the United States.

⬤ Students practice their computer skills at a management training institute in Bangalore.

Employment and Economy

India has one of the largest and most dynamic economies in the world, with industries ranging from traditional village farming to high-tech manufacturing. Over the last ten years, the economy has boomed, but although some Indians have become rich, average incomes in India are still low.

● An employee at a call center in Delhi takes a phone call from a customer. Call-center employees need good language skills and often have to work at night to cater for clients calling from overseas.

Rapid Growth

India's growth dates back to the 1990s, when the government changed the way the economy was organized to encourage businesses to be more competitive. Many foreign companies were attracted by India's low labor costs and set up factories and call centers employing English-speaking workers.

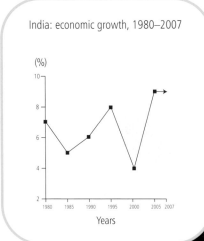

India: economic growth, 1980–2007

(%)

Years

Because India has many highly skilled ICT specialists, it has gained a worldwide reputation for high technology and software development. Bangalore in Karnataka is known as India's Silicon Valley and is the nation's leading IT employer and exporter.

Income Inequality

In 2007, India's GDP reached a record high of $1.1 trillion. But although some Indians have become rich, India's wealth has not been widely shared. The industries that grew the fastest—trade, finance, and services—only employ around 30 percent of the working population. Most Indians work on farms or in workshops or craft-based businesses making goods to sell on the street or in village markets. Many are casual laborers who only work when jobs are available.

Women Workers

Despite government efforts to encourage women to join the work force, only 34 percent of Indian women are in paid employment compared to 82 percent of men. The vast majority work unpaid in the home or on the land.

Because of traditional attitudes, women often find it hard to get well-paid jobs. Sex discrimination is widespread, and women who succeed in getting managerial jobs are rarely paid as much as men.

▶ A woman construction worker carries cement at a building site in Mumbai.

DID YOU KNOW?

With over one million employees, Indian Railroads is the second-largest employer in the world, after the Chinese armed forces.

Facts at a Glance

Economic structure:
 agriculture: 17.2%
 industry: 29.1%
 services: 53.7%

Labor force:
 agriculture: 60%
 industry: 12%
 services: 28%

Female labor force:
 28.1% of total

Unemployment rate: 6.8%

Industry and Trade

India's industrial output is rising steadily. In the past, the government tried to keep out foreign competitors by taxing imports, but since the 1990s, most of the barriers have been lifted and India now has trading links with countries all over the world.

Key Industries

India has always been a farming nation, and agriculture employs more people than any other sector. Recently, however, industries such as iron and steel and a growing software and service sector have replaced agriculture as India's main source of wealth.

Other important industries include textiles, chemicals, food processing, transportation equipment, cement, mining of ores and metals, and oil and gasoline.

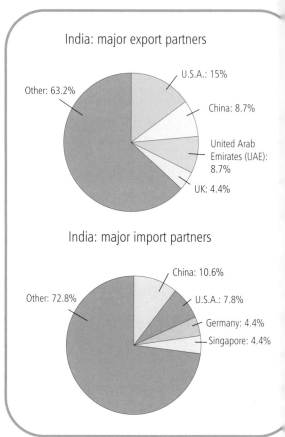

India: major export partners

- Other: 63.2%
- U.S.A.: 15%
- China: 8.7%
- United Arab Emirates (UAE): 8.7%
- UK: 4.4%

India: major import partners

- Other: 72.8%
- China: 10.6%
- U.S.A.: 7.8%
- Germany: 4.4%
- Singapore: 4.4%

Women workers assemble cell phones at a factory in Chennai.

Processing and Manufacturing

A number of India's heavy industries are concentrated in the Chota Nagpur plateau, where there are good supplies of raw materials such as coal and iron ore. Factories that produce consumer goods are mostly based in large cities. Often factory rents are kept low to attract companies to provide jobs for local people.

Energy Needs

As India's economy expands, its energy needs are growing. Most of India's electricity is produced by coal-fired power plants or by hydroelectric plants in the mountains. Twenty-five percent of India's oil comes from the offshore Mumbai High Field and from Gujarat and Assam. Coal comes from some 500 mines scattered over a number of states. A small amount of electricity is generated by nuclear plants.

Imports and Exports

In spite of the growth of recent years, the volume of India's foreign trade is still low. In 2008, imports exceeded exports by a record $93.9 billion.

Since 2000, engineering products have become India's leading export, followed by chemicals, food and agricultural products, gems and jewelry, and leather goods. The main imports include petroleum and petroleum products, precious metals, and chemical products.

Indian silks and cottons are exported to many other countries. The colorful cloths shown here are used as saris, the loose-fitting robes worn by Indian women.

Cars such as the low-cost, energy-efficient Tata Nano are helping India's automobile industry to become one of the most successful and fastest-growing in the world.

DID YOU KNOW? The world's cheapest car is made by the Indian manufacturer Tata. Costing just $2,000, the Tata Nano (right) aims to make driving affordable to millions of Indian people.

Farming and Food

In India, the proportion of land used for farming is greater than almost any other country. The most fertile parts of the country are the Ganges Plain and the deltas of the eastern coast, where almost 90 percent of the land is used for growing.

A Risky Livelihood

Although India's agricultural output is among the highest in the world, Indian farmers have not always been able to grow enough to feed such a large population. Only about half of Indian farms have irrigation systems to water their crops, and few farmers can afford expensive tractors and mechanized equipment.

Facts at a Glance

Farmland: 57% of total land area

Main agricultural exports: rice, cake of soybeans, cashews

Main agricultural imports: palm oil, soy oil, cashews

Average daily calorie intake: 2,440 calories

⬇ A farmer and his wife till a field with a plow drawn by oxen in a remote village in Maharashtra.

Food Crops

In areas where there is enough rain, or where land is irrigated, rice is grown in vast quantities. Wheat is grown mainly on the fertile soils of northern and northwestern India. Legumes such as lentils and chickpeas are the next most important food crop. Most Indians either cannot afford meat or choose not to eat it for religious reasons, so legumes are a major source of protein.

Fertilizers and Pesticides

Since the 1960s, the Indian government has worked hard to promote modern farming methods. During the 1970s, farmers were encouraged to switch to new types of seeds and to use fertilizers to boost production. In the north of the country, crop yields increased dramatically. In other areas, results were mixed.

Use of fertilizers has helped to make the country self-sufficient in wheat and rice and prevented large-scale food shortages. However, in areas such as the Punjab, long-term use of chemicals has reduced the natural goodness in the soil that helps crops to grow. Farmers who have sprayed their crops with pesticides are also having to deal with new, more resistant types of bugs.

A Varied Diet

The typical Indian diet relies heavily on chickpeas, lentils, rice, yogurt, and root vegetables. Indian food is often hot, spicy, and strongly flavored, and traditional dishes such as Madras curry and chicken tikka marsala are popular all over the world.

Favorite foods are *chaats* (savory snacks), *vada paus* (a type of potato sandwich), and samosas, a savory pastry with a filling of spiced potatoes, onion, peas, and cilantro.

An Indian worker picks tea leaves at a plantation. India grows around 31 percent of the world's tea and is also the world's largest tea-drinking nation.

Transportation and Communications

As India's economy has grown, its transportation systems have lagged behind. The government is currently working on a major plan to improve India's road network, but India's cities are often congested, trains and buses are crowded, and delays at India's ports slow down foreign trade.

Getting Around

Most people rely on buses, trains, bicycles, or walking to get around. Several Indian cities including Mumbai, Chennai, Kolkata, Delhi, and Hyderabad now have "rapid transit" train systems. For short, local trips, people also use motorized rickshaws, known as "tuk-tuks."

In rural areas, people often walk or cycle long distances, but in the rainy season, many of India's rural roads can only be used by trucks and SUVs.

DID YOU KNOW?
Although India has only 1 percent of the world's motor vehicles, road accidents in India account for 8 percent of road traffic deaths worldwide.

India's huge "Golden Quadrilateral" highway connects Delhi, Mumbai, Kolkata, and Chennai. The completed highway network will link major cities throughout India.

Facts at a Glance

Total roads: 2.1 milion miles (3.3 million km)

Railroads: 39,284 miles (63,221 km)

Major airports: 70

Major ports: 9

Long-Distance Travel

The Indian train network is one of the busiest in the world, transporting over 18 million passengers and more than 2 million tons of freight every day. The railroads span the length and breadth of the country, covering 6,909 stations over a total network of more than 39,000 miles (63,000 km).

Air travel is expanding, but as more and more people travel by plane, the extra demand puts severe strain on major airports, especially Delhi and Mumbai, which account for around 50 percent of India's air traffic.

India also has a large network of canals and rivers, but only a few waterways in Goa, West Bengal, Assam, and Kerala are used for cargo transportation.

○ Delhi's rapid transit rail system was the second of its kind in India, after Kolkata. Each train can carry up to 240 seated and 400 standing passengers.

Broadcasting and Communications

Since the government started to encourage businesses to be more competitive, many new commercial broadcasting channels have been created in India. These offer everything from soap operas and gameshows to 24-hour news. The public service broadcaster Doordarshan operates 21 services, and its flagship DD1 channel reaches nearly 20 percent of the population.

In 2000, less than 1 percent of Indian households had access to the Internet, but Internet use has risen steeply, with 200 million people accessing the Internet in 2007. Cell phones have also become hugely popular and are an important way for people to keep in touch, especially in remote areas where there are no telephone landlines.

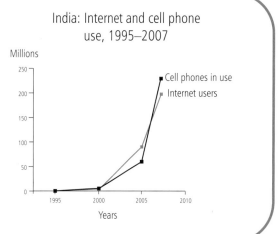

India: Internet and cell phone use, 1995–2007

Millions

- Cell phones in use
- Internet users

Years

Leisure and Tourism

When they are not working, most Indians like to spend time relaxing with friends and family. Reading and watching television are popular, and cheap movie theater tickets mean that the latest Bollywood movies are seen by millions of Indian fans.

Art and Culture

Indian music ranges from classical ragas performed on traditional instruments, to modern pop music influenced by American-style hip-hop and rap. Theater and dance are popular, and plays are often based on stories drawn from Hindu mythology.

Facts at a Glance

Tourist arrivals (millions)

Year	Arrivals
1995	2.1
2000	2.6
2005	3.9
2006	4.4
2007	4.9

▼ Built by Mughal Emperor Shah Jahan in 1648 as a memorial to his wife, the Taj Mahal in Agra, Uttar Pradesh, is one of the most popular tourist sites in the world, attracting 2.4 million visitors in 2007.

India also has produced many internationally famous writers, and the authors Arundhati Roy, Vikram Seth, and Salman Rushdie were all born in India.

Bollywood

India's film industry is the largest in the world, making over 900 films a year. Bollywood studios in Mumbai make commercial movies for Hindi and Urdu speakers that are shown to huge audiences both in India and abroad. There are also successful regional film industries in southern India and Bengal.

Visiting India

India has a thriving tourist industry. People come from all over the world to visit sites such as the Taj Mahal and the Red fortress in Agra, as well as to observe India's rich wildlife. In 2007, nearly 5 million people visited India, spending almost $7.7 billion. Goa, on the Indian west coast, is a popular tourist destination and is renowned for its beaches and architecture.

Sports

Indians are avid followers of sports, and many sports and games, including chess, wrestling, and archery, are thought to have originated in India.

Although India's official national sport is hockey, cricket is the most popular sport and is followed by millions. The national team won the 2007 World Twenty20 cup, and shared the 2002 ICC Champions Trophy with Sri Lanka. All the world's top cricketers take part in the Indian Premier League, which features high-profile, one-day matches screened around the world.

◔ Spectacular song and dance routines and romantic story lines have made Bollywood movies popular with Hindi audiences all over the world.

DID YOU KNOW?
Snakes and ladders was invented in India in the thirteenth century and was called "Mokshapat." In the game, the ladders represented virtues and the snakes stood for vices.

Environment and Wildlife

Elephants, lions, tigers, the one-horned rhinoceros, different types of deer, and huge numbers of rare birds are all found in India. Many of the most endangered species are now preserved in parks and wildlife sanctuaries.

Protection and Conservation

For decades, human activity has threatened India's wildlife. In 1972, a special project was launched to save the Bengal tiger, which had been hunted almost to extinction. As a result, there are now more than 27 tiger sanctuaries across the country, as well as 90 national parks where landscapes, plants, and animals are conserved and protected.

The Bengal tiger was once found throughout the Indian subcontinent. The current population is thought to be around 1,500. One of the main causes of the decline is hunting for skins and for Chinese medicine.

Pressures on the Environment

The pressures of feeding a growing population mean that the environment in India has suffered. Land has been overgrazed and deforested to plant crops, and irrigation projects have led to water being pumped out of the ground faster than the monsoon rains can replace it.

The growth of the Indian economy has also led to a large increase in air pollution from factories and motor vehicles. Diseases caused by poor air quality are on the increase, and in Bangalore, up to 50 percent of children suffer from asthma, thought to be caused by car exhaust fumes.

Many birds of prey like this white-bellied eagle have seen their hunting grounds destroyed by the rapid spread of India's cities.

Global Warming

Over the years, many of India's low-lying regions have suffered from flooding. As sea levels rise due to global warming, the threat to areas such as east Bengal is becoming greater.

In 2008, the Indian government launched a National Action Plan on Climate Change to reduce the country's dependence on fossil fuels. One of its showcase projects has been a wind farm at Muppandal in Tamil Nadu, where huge turbines now tower over the palm trees. The farm has been so successful that many others have been set up in the area, and thousands of jobs have been created for local people.

Solar power also has great potential for the future, and could supply the needs of millions of Indians who live in remote villages that are not connected to the national energy grid.

Solar panels being assembled in a factory in Rajasthan. The panels are for export to other countries and also for domestic use in India, where solar power is helping to bring electricity to remote villages for the first time.

Glossary

bamboo lightweight but strong wood used for poles

call center centralized office where employees answer phone calls from customers

caste social group into which Hindus are born

climate normal weather conditions of an area

compulsory something you must do

culture way of life and traditions of a particular group of people

delta landform at the mouth of a river

economy the way that trade and money are controlled by a country

empire group of countries controlled by a single, more powerful nation

export good or service that is sold to another country

extended family family including grandparents, uncles, aunts, and cousins as well as parents, brothers, and sisters

federal (of country) made up of several states or regions

fertile good for growing crops, especially in large quantities

garland wreath of flowers worn around the neck

GDP Gross Domestic Product: the total value of goods and services produced by a country

hydroelectricity power generated by falling or fast-moving water

import good or service that is bought from another country

innoculate to protect against disease and infection

intermarriage marriage between people who belong to different ethnic groups

literacy being able to read and write

malnourished lacking the food and vitamins that are needed to grow and thrive

managerial job that involves organizing work of other people

matchmaker person who arranges for two people to meet and/or get married

monopoly when one organization controls the supply of a good or service

monsoon type of wind that brings rain when blowing from the southwest

natural resources raw materials such as wood and minerals that are found in a country

nuclear energy released by a nuclear reaction

nuclear family "core" family group, usually consisting of father, mother, and child(ren)

peninsula piece of land projecting into the sea

pharmaceuticals drugs used for medical treatment

pilgrim person who makes a trip to a holy place

populous containing many people

republic system of government in which people elect officials to make decisions on their behalf

rural to do with the countryside or agriculture

sanitation facilities for washing and disposing of sewage

sector a division of something such as a type of industry

secular not religious

shanty town area where poor people live, often found on the outskirts of large cities

shrine holy place devoted to a god or a person

siblings brothers and sisters

species animals or plants that share common features

subcontinent land forming a large part of a continent

textiles fabric or cloth

unemployment being without paid work

urban to do with towns and town life

vaccine medicine used to protect against an infectious disease

Topic Web

Use this topic web to explore Indian themes in different areas of your curriculum.

IT
Imagine you are planning a vacation in India. Use the Internet to help you to decide where to go and what to see.

Geography
India is the largest English-speaking nation in the world. Find out which other countries speak the English language and shade them on a world map.

Science
India is rich in many natural resources such as coal. Find out how coal is made, and what problems are thought to be caused by burning fossil fuels such as coal.

Math
Many important features of the number system were invented by Indian mathematicians centuries ago. Find out what some of these were. What would math be like without them?

India

English
Find out about the Indian authors mentioned on page 27. What kind of books do they write? Where in India were they born? Where do they live and work now?

Citizenship
India is a member of the Commonwealth of Nations. Find out more about the Commonwealth. How many countries are members? What are some of the advantages of being in the Commonwealth?

History
India is one of the world's oldest civilizations. Find out more about the ancient origins of India, dating back to 3000 BCE and beyond.

Design and Technology
The Taj Mahal at Agra was built as a monument to a special person. Imagine you have been asked to design a monument for somebody important. What would it look like?

Further Information, Web Sites, and Index

Further reading

A World Of Recipes: India by Julie McCulloch (Heinemann Raintree, 2009)
Looking At Countries: Looking At India by Jillian Powell (Gareth Stevens Publishing, 2007)
World In Focus: Focus On India by Ali Brownlie Bojang and Nicola Barber (Gareth Stevens Publishing, 2006)

Web Sites

Due to the changing nature of Internet links, PowerKids Press has developed an online list of Web sites related to the subject of this book. This site is updated regularly. Please use this link to access this list:
http://www.powerkidslinks.com/discovc/india/

Index